I AM WORTHY

Showing Your Self-Worth And Self-Confidence

By

Ana Rita Reyes

By Ana Rita Reyes

ISBN:

Hardbound-978-621-470-357-9

Softbound/Paperback-978-621-470-466-8

MOBI/KINDLE-978-621-470-359-3

Published by:

Poetry Planet Book Publishing House

Rosario, Pozorrubio, Pangasinan, Philippines

Contact Number: 09554960094

Email: maritesritumalta@gmail.com

PREFACE

This book has a simple purpose of sharing the wisdom of giving importance to knowing thyself, loving our own life, and understanding our self-worth. To act, think, speak, and say well is the most salient aspect of self-love and self-worth.

It is not about being over indulgence of ourselves but it is seeing yourself as a reflection of how God made us and our purpose. This book wishes to empathize with people who struggle on understanding themselves that is why they are caught in a compromising situation and concerns in life.

When you know yourself better, when you love yourself, and you see your worth you live a life with wholeness and bliss.

FOREWORD

Humans are entitled to dignity and this character is best shown in loving our neighbor the way we love ourselves.

The first person who loves us authentically is God. That is why with His love we will transform it into loving our family, neighbors, benefactors, and our country. And to practice this kind of love that God has expressed to us it must transcend to our neighbor. We must realize that our first neighbor is ourselves. St. Thomas Aquinas stressed that the path of loving others begins with loving ourselves. However, the basis of this love does not dwell on vainglory and self-serving but on the criteria of the commandment of Jesus Christ that we must love one another as He has loved us.

This book will exemplify the importance of self-care and self-love to attain a level of self-worth by rediscovering our lost fullness and awareness.

TABLE OF CONTENTS

Self-love is when you embrace your humanness according to how God created you by our complete obedience to His will to achieve the fullness of life.

Understanding Self-Love And Self-Worth

Being good is not enough to know your worth and how you express your love to God, to self and to neighbors. The genuine expression of self-love and self-worth comes from the teaching of Jesus to "Love one another, as He has loved us". This must be our deep principle and our guiding source of inspiration in living a life of wholeness.

As we live our life and we interact with people there must be a level of worthiness that we need to rediscover. This level of worthiness will be our guide and our preference about who our first neighbor is and where our loyalty, love and care must begin and transcend. When we follow these set of guidelines, seeing our worth, expression of our care and love will be distributed fairly, just and equal.

Who is our neighbor?

1st Neighbor: God and Church

2nd Neighbor: Self

3rd Neighbor: Family (Single) Spouse and Children (Married)

4th Neighbor: Relatives

5th Neighbor: Friends & Benefactor

6th Neighbor: Country and Countrymen

This guideline will help us prioritize our way of giving, kindness, and priority in setting our decisions and plans. For example, you have to prioritize your commitment to your husband and children over your siblings if you are married, the same way that your obligation to your country, countrymen (stranger) must never go beyond your care to your friends and benefactors. Knowing these guidelines will help you identify your priority without jeopardizing any relationship based on facts and order. This is the natural order that God want to see in us and this is the order that we must follow so that we live in harmony with our mind, body, and spirit.

Physical Care Is Health Care

CHAPTER I:

Physical Care Is Self-Care

"If you don't make time for your wellness, you will be forced to make time for your illness" a tweet from @wealth_director

To heal and be strong from the inside, we must first clean what is outside. In the Bible, Jesus expressed His words to His disciple Matthew 26:41 "Watch and pray, that ye enter not into temptation: the spirit indeed is willing, but the flesh is weak." In this context Jesus is telling us that we must take care of the body as a temple of the Holy Ghost and we have to make sure that our body is able and capable and ready for any battle.

Since our body is a gift from God we must use it for good purposes and we must never abuse or exclude its personal needs. We are created to bear divine image thus we must always have a receptive recognition of this grace so that our action and purpose of this God's given body will be employed for a higher purpose which is to unite with God's will and for the service of neighbor.

Sleeping 8-10 hours a day, water intake, avoiding overconsumption, limiting our sugar and salt intake, removing vices, proper hygiene, recreation, and avoiding stress are some of the tips that can ensure that you will live in wellness that is fit and right. We can't compromise the needs of our bodies because they will be our powerful instrument in our day-to-day journey in life. Our endeavor and task need our vigor, body and strength. Having a frail and feeble body will hamper the succession of our tasks and goals.

Our first neighbor is ourselves, that is why physical health, emotional soundness, mental fitness, and spiritual adeptness must proceed from ourselves first and then slowly transcend to our next neighbor which is our family, followed by our relatives, friends, benefactors, and countrymen.

The National Catholic Register on their website (ncregister.com) summarized 5 ways to Holiness that requires taking care of our body.

First is "Sound hygiene is almost an intellectual virtue. Among our moderns, whose philosophy is sometimes so poor, the science of hygiene is rich; do not despise it; it will enrich your philosophy." This focuses on hygiene and being spic and span in our body.

The second is "Live as much as possible in the open air. It is a recognized fact that attention … is closely related to breathing, and for general health, we know that plenty of oxygen is the first condition. Windows open or partly open day and night when prudence allows, frequent deep breathing exercises, combined with movements that amplify them and make them normal, walk before and after work, or even combined with work according to the Greek tradition; all these practices are excellent." This entails our habits that can bring wellness in a holistic way such as getting fresh air, good recreation, and activities that bring vitality.

The third is "Look after your diet. Light food, plain, moderate in quantity, and simply cooked, will enable you to work more freely and alertly. A thinker does not spend his life in the process of digestion." You are what you eat. Remember that overconsumption is gluttony which is the sister sin of lust because it indulges in pleasure and aberration and is a scapegoat for reality.

The fourth is "Every day you should exercise. Remember the saying of an English doctor: 'Those who do not find time to take exercise must find time to be ill.'"

And the fifth is "Pay still more attention to your sleep. Take neither too much nor too little. Too much will make you heavy, stupid, will slow up the blood and the power of thinking; too little will expose you to the risk of prolonging unduly the stimulation of work and dangerously superimposing strain upon the strain." Many deaths are caused by sleep deprivation.

Taking care of our body has a wide range. Aside from it helps to bolster our immune system, it also aids us to attune our body, mind, and soul. (National Catholic Register)

Peace Over Stress Is Self-care

CHAPTER 2

Peace Over Stress Is Self- Care

Stress is the new plague

Stress is the reason why productive and creative people lose their sheen and luster. This debilitating factor in our life can destroy our health, emotion, mental sharpness, and even our relationship to our sphere.

Stress according to UN News "Stress, over time, disease, contribute to 2.8 million workers' deaths per year, reports UN labor agency". This is alarming because we thought that stress is just a form of burnout or anxiety but it is indeed a disorder that increases the risk and possibility of acquiring or worsening diseases such as autoimmune diseases, diabetes, cancers, and other metabolic ailment.

Stress makes us lethargic, destroys our focus, makes us restless, and gives us a lack of sleep eventually can alleviate serious physical, emotional, and mental maladies.

Tough situations, hard dealing with people, and personal problems can be consuming but if we know how to channel stress into motivation we can change the direction of our life. Every problem has a solution and if there is no solution we have to accept that it is the truth. Acceptance of the truth is the key to freedom from anxiety. We can be eager about the new beginning by looking for a new quest or something to throw off but not as a scapegoat. But instead, as a journey towards liberty from stress and discomfort.

When you recognize that you need change instead of resisting it you are learning not only emotional quotient or maturity but you are acquiring Adversity quotient. Adversity quotient is the ability to live and deal with any ordeal and trials in life. In a spiritual aspect, it is called " Holy Indifference". Holy Indifference is a state wherein a person is detached from the world and attached to the will of God. It is the total openness to the will of God thus any trials, hardship, and suffering can't shake you anymore because you believe that everything that happens in your life and the world is allowed by God and has a good and advantageous purpose even if we can't understand it. That is the beauty of God's mystery. We can't fathom His will and plan but it will assure us and it's strengthening us.

Always focus on your goal. Aim for a healthier and happier life and do not let distraction and trouble stir you down and put you into trouble. When you feel overwhelmed you must stop, relax, and recreate. Program your mind that there are various remedies available instead of succumbing to stress and anxiety.

Get into prayer, meditation, and time of silence to clear your thoughts and allow God to feed you with hope. The burden is not what God wants for us, he wanted us to experience joy and despite we have some concerns, he guarantees and assures us that His presence will always be with us until the end of times to lift us and help us because He loves us, we only need to ask Him in our day to day life.

There are practical ways to relieve stress and embrace peace of mind.

1. Always focus on what you can change and learn to accept what you can't.
2. In every situation you have to choose to respond rather than react. The response is always moving towards logical and tactful responsibility in addressing a concern, while the reaction is driven by emotion and the subconscious.
3. Spend time to be alone and in prayer. The more you put yourself into silence and being alone the more you gain wisdom and serenity Of the mind and soul. Prayer is always the action of the strong because it teaches you humility while giving you the power to move forward efficiently with courage and precision.
4. Have a habit of writing in a journal. Whatever happens to your day, write down the learnings that you discover. Writing a positive note will improve your ability to be patient and hopeful.
5. Always manage your expectations. People, situations, and events in our life. Sometimes expecting too much can incapacitate us. That is why learning to change our expectations and reframing by accepting that irregularities can happen is teaching us a lesson.

Peace is a grace from God and we must use this grace to overcome stress and downpours in life.

Give and Forgive Is Self-Care

CHAPTER 3

To Give And Forgive Is Self-Care

God doesn't want to see us carrying heavy burdens and He wants us to release all the bitterness, hatred, and resentment that is lurking in our hearts. Forgiveness is an emancipating experience wherein trust and love are beginning to grow in our souls again.

Yes, indeed, it is hard to forgive when we are deeply wounded but by accepting the virtue of humility, slowly our hearts will be softened and will have the transforming courage to offer forgiveness. Without forgiveness, our hearts and souls become corrosive and will bring us to degeneration and emotional disaster.

Forgiveness is the authentic belief that the person who causes harm to us is also loved by God and we must offer our prayer and blessings to those who prey on us because of our love for God and our willing desire to be liberated from ill feelings and any evil attachment.

Forgiveness is always neglected among us but it is a salient virtue, it brings back joy, reclaims our entirety, and allows grace to flow into our life, works, and our relationships.

When we forgive we obtain peace while we joyfully give out love. It brings harmony and wipes the influence of wounds in our hearts.

To let go of one's painful memory of the past frees the heart from resentment and hatred that we have bottled up for a very long time. However, the process is far from easy, especially when we are reminded of our mistakes daily. That feeling of immense guilt will continue to linger if we choose to continue blaming ourselves for something we cannot change anymore. Whenever we look back at destructive habits we did a long time ago, the embarrassment, shame, and negative perception of the self-culminate in locking ourselves in a cage.

As Robin Sharma said "Stop being a prisoner of your past, Become the architect of your future.", we are not granted the luxury of having a time machine that would've allowed us to avoid committing those sins had we acted differently, we are human and it is inevitable.

The only way we can forgive ourselves for our past actions is to accept the fact that we are flawed. We can start by becoming accountable for our errors instead of escaping, face them and acknowledge the faulty things we did and how (bad) they affected the people that were involved. Then genuinely seek for forgiveness the people who got hurt and most importantly yourself.

"The first step to forgiveness is forgiving yourself first"

Forgive yourself for being involved in a bad romance but love yourself for escaping from that emotional tragedy. Forgive yourself for failure but love yourself each time you surpass every struggle. Forgive yourself for being cheated but love yourself for overcoming betrayal. Forgive yourself for being unfortunate but love yourself for the history of your journey that makes you complete.

Forgive yourself for failures but love yourself for your every achievement. Forgive people when they judge you but love them when they learn that they were wrong. Forgive your destiny for being unfortunate but love your journey for you are making wonderful history...

Forgiveness Prayer For Adults

By: Fr. Robert DeGrandis, S.S.J. (1932-2018)

In the following prayer, most of the significant areas will be covered. Often such a prayer will bring to mind other areas that need forgiveness. Let the Holy Ghost move freely and guide your mind to persons or groups that you need to forgive.

Lord Jesus Christ, I ask today to forgive everyone in my life. I know that You will give me strength to forgive and I thank You that You love me more than I love myself and want my happiness more than I desire it for myself.

Lord Jesus, I want to be free from the feelings of resentment, bitterness, and unforgiveness toward You for the times I thought You sent death, hardships, financial difficulties, punishments, and sickness in our family.

Lord, I forgive myself for my sins, faults, and failings. For all that is truly bad in me or all that I think is bad, I do forgive myself. For a delving in the occult, Ouija boards, horoscopes, seances, fortune telling, lucky charms, [dream catchers]; for taking my name in vain; for not worshiping You; for hurting my parents; for getting drunk; [for the use of illegal drugs]; [for the misuse of legal drugs]; for sins against my purity; for adultery; for abortion; for stealing; for lying — I am truly forgiving myself today. Thank You, Lord, for Your grace at this moment.

I truly forgive my mother. I forgive her for all the times she hurt me, resented me, was angry with me and for all the times she punished me [unjustly]. I forgive her for the times she preferred my brothers and sisters to me. I forgive her for the times she told me I was dumb, ugly, stupid, the worst of the children or that I cost the family a lot of money. For the times she told me I was unwanted, an accident, a mistake, or not what she expected. [For any negativity, gossip, manipulation, or bad example], I forgive her.

I forgive my father. I forgive him for a lack of support, any lack of love, affection, or attention. I forgive him for any lack of time, for not giving me his companionship, for his drinking or arguing and fighting with my mother or other children. For his severe punishments, for desertion, for being away from home, for divorcing my mother, or for any running around, I do forgive him.

(The forgiveness for mother and father can be interchangeable depending on your story)

Lord, I extend forgiveness to my sisters and brothers. I forgive those who rejected me, lied about me, hated me, resented me, competed for my parents' love, and those who hurt me, and physically harmed me. For those who were too severe on me, punished me, or made my life unpleasant in any way, I do forgive them.

Lord, I forgive my spouse for lack of love, affection, consideration, support, attention, communication, for faults, failings, weaknesses, and those other acts or words that hurt or disturb me. Jesus, I forgive my children for their lack of respect, obedience, love, attention, support, warmth, understanding; their bad habits, falling away from the Church, and bad actions that disturb me.

My God, I forgive my in-laws—mother, father, son or daughter-in-law, sister, brother-in-law, and other relatives by marriage. For their lack of love, words of criticism, thoughts, actions, or omissions that injure and cause pain, I do forgive them. Please help me to forgive my relatives, my grandmother, and my grandfather who may have interfered in our family, been possessive of my parents, who may have caused confusion or turned one parent against the other.

Jesus, help me to forgive my co-workers who are disagreeable or make life miserable for me. For those who push their work off on me, gossip about me, won't cooperate with me, try to take my job, I do forgive them.

My neighbors need to be forgiven, Lord. For all their noise, letting their property run-down, [not training their pets properly], not taking in their trash cans, being prejudiced and running down the neighborhood, I do forgive them.

I now forgive my clergyman, [ministers], my congregation, and my church for all their lack of support, pettiness, bad sermons, lack of friendliness, not affirming me as they should, not inspire me, for not using me in a key position, for not inviting me to serve in a major capacity and for any other hurt they have inflicted—I do forgive them today.

Lord, I forgive all professional people who have hurt me in any way—doctors, nurses, police officers, hospital workers, lawyers, contractors. For anything they did to me unjustly, I truly forgive them. Lord, I forgive my employer for not paying me enough money, for not appreciating my work, for being unkind and unreasonable with me, for being angry and unfriendly, for not promoting me, and for not complimenting me on my work.

Lord, I forgive my school teachers, professors, and instructors of the past, as to well as the present. For those who punished me, humiliated me, insulted me, treated me unjustly, made fun of me, called me dumb or stupid, or made me stay after school.

Lord, I forgive my friends who have let me down, lost contact with me, do not support me, were not available when I needed help, borrowed money, and did not return it gossiped about me. Lord Jesus, I especially pray for the grace of forgiveness for that one person in life who has hurt me the most. I ask to forgive anyone who I consider my greatest enemy, the one who I said I would never forgive.

Thank You, Jesus, that I am free of the evil of unforgiveness. Let Your Holy Spirit fill me with light and let every dark area of my mind be enlightened.

AMEN.

Remember, forgiveness is an act of will, not a feeling. Jesus calls us to forgive always and throughout our entire lives. Daily we need to forgive those who hurt or injure us. “Then Peter came up and said to him, ‘Lord, how often shall my brother sin against me, and I forgive him? As many as seven times?’ Jesus said to him, ‘I do not say to you seven times, but seventy times seven.” (Matt. 18:21-22, RSV CE).

Silence is Self-Care

CHAPTER 4

Silence Is Self-Care

"Silence Is Gold."

They say that speech is silver yet silence is Gold. When we speak we only discuss what we already know but when we keep ourselves silent and listen, we gain new information and learn. When we integrate and synthesize it in our life it becomes wisdom.

The problem with the world is that all of us are talking and only a few of us are listening. That is why we have a chaotic and confusing life. Instead of communicating and listening, we chose to live interfering. When all of us are discussing, criticizing, and arguing then the truth and certainty are far from us. Because it is only by listening that we learn to agree and concede to what is truthful and apparent.

When we are silent we entrust our thoughts, hearts, and souls to discernment. Discernment is a factual judgment with a good grasp and awareness of what is uncertain. Silent is a voice of the heart and soul that gives clarity, tranquility, and hope.

Silence has a golden effect on us because instead of pointing out our opinion, we channel our energy towards stillness that can give more dignity and equilibrium. When we give people silent treatment it usually gives them the impression that we can live independently and it generates respect and decent audacity. The dignity behind silence has a tremendous effect in that it can soften the hearts of those who are hostile to us, and it gives us a feeling of ease and peace.

Speeches and sermons can be annoying and degrading. This kind of irritation can reduce our concentration and it can give us emotional and physical stress. Talking to someone can be stressful too specifically when we get into a conversation that gives us an overwhelming experience and a bitter feeling. When there are issues in life, it is better that you just handle them alone or seek the right people because often when we share our concerns with others, sometimes unsolicited advice is given to us. Some people are not good at empathy that is there are people whose words are tactless and hurtful that can cause additional wounds than healing.

Silence has a productive and healing effect on the body. According to Healthline Silence may help your health in several ways, including:

- lowering blood pressure
- improving concentration and focus
- calming racing thoughts
- stimulating brain growth
- reducing cortisol
- stimulating creativity
- improving insomnia
- encouraging mindfulness

That is why we have to choose silence because it gives us power by providing us with reinforcement to think, plan and act.

Even when we pray God is not impressed with wordy prayers "And when you are praying, speak not much, as the heathens. For they think that in their much speaking they may be heard." (Matthew 6:7, Douay Rheims) that is why short but efficient prayer must be utter to God to receive His divine will just by saying "Speak to me my Lord, and My God, your servant is listening" Let God speak more and we listen most.

True achievement and
authentic success are
validated by contentment
and kindness..
~Ana Rita Reyes

CHAPTER 5

"Learning To Say That's Enough Is Self-Care"

The common failure of people who are walking toward their dreams is looking at the life and journey of others. That is why some of most people's ambitions do not come into reality because of trying to simulate others' lives. Some may reach their dreams but it is born of exhaustion because the way of attaining those goals is outlined from somebody's life success. That is why because of this way of thinking about success, people tend to overwork, become jaded, and invariably feel deprived.

The reality of success varies from several points of view. For some success is about popularity, richness in resources, and several linkages but for some, it is just about what makes you joyous and satisfied.

Many successful people in the world have everything yet still suffer from emptiness, dissatisfaction, and unhappiness because it seems that the more you have something, the less you appreciate it. You may have all the businesses and great careers but still, you are deprived of time and the care of your family and children because of your busyness. The more you have wealth and popularity the more your sanity, security, love, and belongingness are jeopardized. Trust issues can also be imperiled because you don't know who is truly into you or those who are riding on your success.

When there is a disproportionate outcome of your achievement then it is a false success. Success, according to Steve Rose Ph.D., means living in alignment with your definition of success by staying true to your values and taking meaningful actions toward your own valued goals.

Ideally, success is a grace, it produces contentment and comfort. Genuine success is not made by stress but rather it is a free-flowing blessing as an outcome of smart work and perseverance. True success has no opposing undercurrent but it is just fuelled by hope and positiveness.

Without contentment and satisfaction, success is false. And success is expressed through satisfaction, gratification, and joy in the fulfillment of the mission. "Contentment is one of the most distinguishing traits of the godly person because a godly person has his heart focused on God rather than on possessions or position, or power" Jerry Bridges.

Do not ask God for success and richness, ask him to make you kinder and more generous, once these virtues are strengthened in you, He will supply what you need to be an outlet of grace to others.

EACH TIME YOU WAKE UP IN THE MORNING MAKE IT A HABIT TO SMILE, TO THINK OF GOD, AND TO THINK GOOD. WHATEVER GOOD AND PLEASING THAT YOU SUPPLY IN YOUR THOUGHTS EACH MORNING WILL BE EQUATED TO BLESSINGS.
~Ana Rita Reyes

CHAPTER 6

Positive Thinking Is Self-Care

"Wake Up and Think Great"

It is said that joy always comes in the morning. When you start your day, our first appointment must be God. When we fill our hearts with positivity, contentment, and hope, our days will be recharged and will be blessed.

Each day is a day of possibility. We must never allow our past and trouble to hinder the promise that awaits us. If we are headed towards greatness we must live by faith and determination.

When your heart is full of optimistic reality it will produce encouraging behavior that can inspire and elicit good vibes from others. Our greatness depends on what we maintain in our hearts. If we keep persistence and productivity we gain success, if we fulfill learning then we attain wisdom, if we pursue faith then we can foresee grace.

Each morning is a day to grow, an opportunity to prosper, and a chance to do better and to discover more of your abilities and what you can give more. When you start with what is good for your soul each day, all your work will flourish and you can do the impossible through the blessing of God in your life.

Whatever you wish for becomes your prayer to yourself thus make sure that you are wishing the best for yourself every morning.

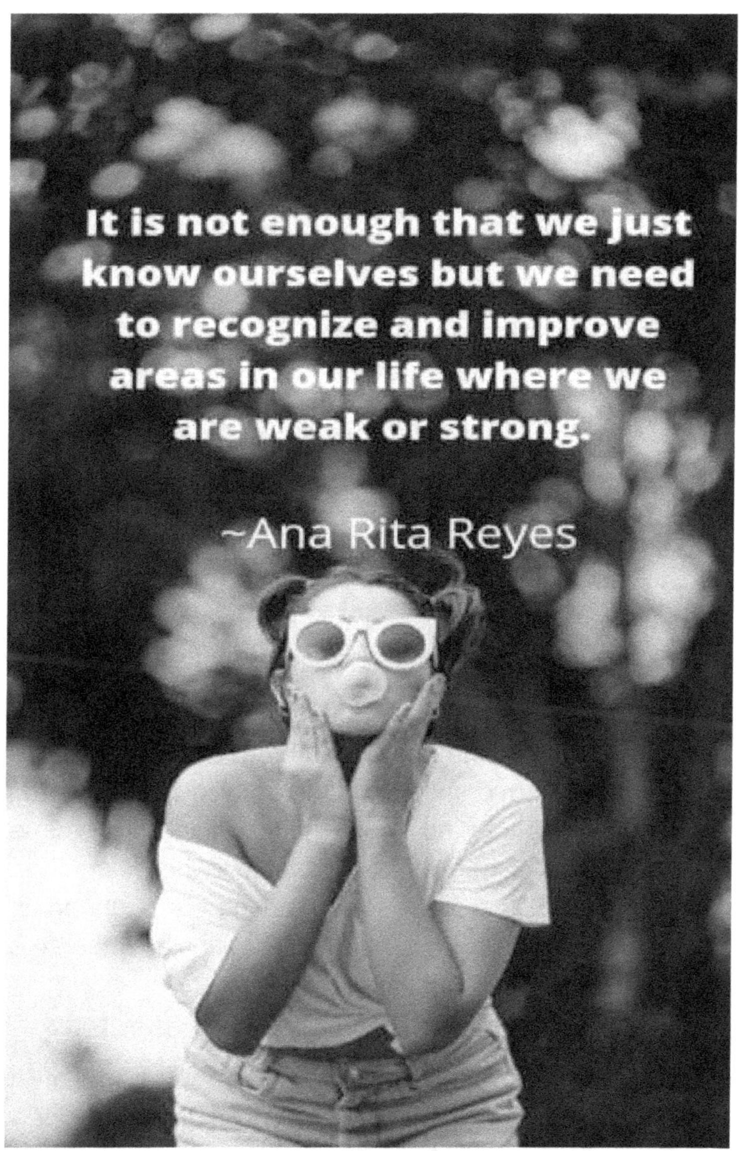

Neutralizing your Temperament is Self-Care

CHAPTER 7

Neutralizing Your Temperament Is Self-Care

"You and Your Inborn Personality"

The common error today is why there are a lot of conflicts and disputes in our home, work, and community. It is because we see everyone as equal and comparable.

We are crying out for equality but we never understood what we truly mean. Each one of us is designed differently. Man and woman differ from one another. Yes, we are equal as God's creation but we are diverse in personality and traits. So we must acknowledge our differences and our traits because if we foster the poor concept of equality then individuality, variousness, and sense of identity will be diminished.

Knowing thyself is a form of intelligence. Since we already have the so-called Multiple Intelligence we must understand that learning and understanding ourselves is Intrapersonal Intelligence. If we truly know who we are then we can truly take care of our space, and our boundaries, and we can modify our extent and limitations based on the right, liberty, and personal space of others.

How do we know ourselves? It depends on God's given personality that is encoded in use. You will identify if you are a Choleric, Sanguine, Melancholic Phlegmatic personality or mixed of this temperament by taking some Temperament tests available on the internet. Through recognizing and knowing your temperament and someone's temperament you will find out how to respond appropriately and learn to coexist in peace and understanding with your family, spouse, children, and neighbor. The idea of human personality is based on Hippocrates and it is adapted widely to discern ourselves so that we can connect and appreciate other people's reactions and responses towards us and to a certain situation. Our behavior and responses are based on our innate temperament. Knowing ourselves based on temperaments can help us identify our boundaries, our strength, and areas of weakness so that we can express empathy, care, and buoyant relationships with our family, spouse, children, workmate, and fellow men.

Strong temperaments such as Choleric who are domineering, born as leaders, highly confident, and goal-oriented must be propelled by humility and patience because this kind of personality can be intimidating and can wound people so bad because this identity demands goals and one's you are directed to your goal you become unstoppable without realizing that you have hurt people just to hit your target. However, if you know that you have a Choleric personality and you know how to handle its strength and weakness you will realize that you are living with a heart of Success. For a Sanguine who loves fun, has optimistic views, and can easily forgive, if a person doesn't know how this personality works they will end up having a problem with focus and impulsiveness. That is why we can see people who keep on shifting from different jobs to another job and have problems with commitment and relationships because of this personality trait. If you appreciate your sanguine personality you will gain friendships and your heart is moved by joy so you will learn the virtue of persistence and bind on responsibility. People with Melancholic personalities are detailed, creative, and thoughtful. Yet, with this personality, they always aim for perfection, and if you can't withstand their desire for quintessence they can easily lose their trust and confidence in you. Having this personality must be guarded because aside from being introverts, they are prone to depression, mood swings, procrastination, being obsessive, and too cautious. On a lighter note, their heart aims for precision that is why they are full of wisdom. And the last temperament is the Phlegmatic who is peace-loving, diplomatic, quiet, and calm. Their weakness pertains to being prone to laziness, too compromising, and being non-participative. Learning the Phlegmatic personality will be valuable as good mediation because of your agreeable resolution through good listening and being highly intuitive.

The door to having a good relationship and a healthy connection to people around us is based on our values and strength by truly knowing ourselves first. Let us be clear that our life must not be entangled with other people's values and character because our identity must always come from the personality that is conceived of us. If we don't know ourselves our path will be doubtful and it will ruin our joy.

When we recognize and
understand our love
language and others' love
language, surely
negativity and hate will
not progress in our home
and community.
~Ana Rita Reyes

CHAPTER 8

Avoiding Toxic People Is Self-Care

"It's my rule, it's my space"

Peace of mind is when your mind, heart, and soul experience serenity, calmness, and ease. This priceless experience brings natural joy and fullness to our daily life. We must realize that our God's given passion and appetite for creativity, ideation, and aptitude can only flow steadily if we express our humanness in an environment where love, compassion, and appreciation are being promoted and nurtured.

However, no matter how we try to reach out and bestow kindness to people in our work and people we meet each day, there are circumstances that we can observe that some individuals are not really into us. There are a few situations where finding good friendship is not possible, hostile or unpleasant treatment can be projected upon us even if we are nonchalant and do nothing towards anyone know. This is a red flag that must be considered and it is an apparent reason to avoid and forgo this kind of toxicity.

Toxic people are those who play victim, rationalize mistakes, are gossipers, manipulators, exaggerate when they defend themselves, always get jealous, usually do power-tripping, and sometimes make you feel guilty even though they are the ones who are doing the wrongdoings. Being knotted with these people can wreck your emotional health and can deplete your spirit. Since we can't change them, the best remedy is to avoid and ignore them but to continue being kind to them as necessary. We must channel our effort to sustain our productivity instead of satisfying and changing them.

People are not intrinsically bad, instead, they are merely wounded, that is why we must understand and discern the pattern of their inimical behavior. The Bioecological theory formulated by Urie Bronfenbrenner suggests that an individual has a different environmental sphere that affects the development and behavioral pattern thus, every environmental sphere has a favorable or adverse consequence on a person's manner.

Sometimes, people we talk to like our family members, co-workers, friends, and strangers could give us ill-feelings. Unfortunately, there is a situation where those who are in close relationship with us are the one who is expressing havoc behavior toward us and it can be discomforting. Giving up on them is not an option however we can express respectful disagreement without engaging in accusations but by discussing the fact, talking about their behavior, and coming up with a wholesome solution. Expressing to them without judgment about their toxic behavior may benefit them in acknowledging that their demeanor is not acceptable.

In an occurrence where a friend or co-worker is making it hard on you, you have to protect yourself first instead of your relationship with that person. The Healthline website suggests that "Taking care of yourself involves making sure you have enough emotional energy to meet your own needs. This may not happen when you're giving everything to someone who doesn't offer anything in return."

Avoiding toxic people is not a form of weakness, instead it is a form of wisdom. Sometimes we are not dealing with people but with the terrible character that they possess. Ignoring the poor behavior of others is the best gift we can offer for our mental health. Standing on your ground when someone tries to suffocate you with their awful behavior means courage. When people see that you are disinclined with your peculiar behavior they will learn to set boundaries and will avoid taunting you.

You can mute people in real life too... It's called boundaries. (anonymous)

On Twitter, @Resilientthuman has furnished 14 ways to handle difficult/toxic people without driving yourself crazy.

1. State your Intentions Up-front

- ✓ Manage expectations upfront.
- ✓ Tell them how bringing this topic up makes you uncomfortable.
- ✓ And tell them that it's important to discuss this anyway.
- ✓ When you set expectations in this way, the conversations go much more smoothly.

2. Use Inclusive Language

- ✓ When you lead with accusations like "You always" and "You never" the walls go up.
- ✓ To stop this, start your statements with "I" and "We".

"I felt hurt".

"I felt misunderstood".

- ✓ It stops the situation from escalating and allows communication.

3. Steer Clear of Absolutes

- ✓ Words like "always" and "never" are trigger words.
- ✓ It blows the conversation out of proportion.
- ✓ And it leads to the other person finding an exception and more defensiveness.
- ✓ Best to stay away from them.

4. Stick to the Facts

- ✓ Be very specific about what upset you.
- ✓ Talk about the precise chain of events that led to it.
- ✓ Do not generalize.
- ✓ And do not interpret their intentions.
- ✓ When you do that, it leads to defensiveness.

5. Ask Questions

- ✓ Ask open-ended questions.
- ✓ Open up the floor for them.
- ✓ Ask them if anything you said or did trigger them.
- ✓ It keeps the conversation moving.
- ✓ It also gives them a chance to explain what prompted their strong response.

6. Stay Aware of *Emotion*

- ✓ Keep a steady finger on your emotional pulse.
- ✓ When dealing with difficult people, your buttons will get pushed.

- ✓ So if you're not aware of your emotional state, you will be prone to fly off the handle.

7. Do not Mirror Anger

- ✓ When tempers flare up, it's easy to get carried away with anger.
- ✓ But recognize and stop when you are mirroring the other person's anger.
- ✓ Even if you feel attacked, stay calm.
- ✓ Giving in to anger only snowballs the situation and leads to regret.

8. Don't let them get Under your Skin

- ✓ During difficult interactions, it's natural that tempers will flare.
- ✓ And accusations will get thrown at you.
- ✓ But never let them get under your skin.
- ✓ You are the only person who gets to decide your truth.

9. Set Limits

- ✓ Decide what kind of behavior you would tolerate from the other person.
- ✓ If things are getting out of hand, raise your hand towards the other person with an open palm.
- ✓ Signal them to stop.
- ✓ If you feel it necessary, use definitive statements with the gesture.
- ✓ "Please don't use that tone with me," or "Please don't talk to me this way."
- ✓ This gesture creates separation.

- ✓ And it creates a message that cannot be fought with words.

10. Take a Break

- ✓ If things are getting too heated, take a 20-minute break.
- ✓ Remove yourself from the room.
- ✓ Tell them "Why don't we take a breather to clear our heads and then come back?"
- ✓ This kind of inclusive language always helps.

11. Reward and Recognize good Behavior

- ✓ When working with somebody is difficult it's very hard to think about rewarding them.
- ✓ But try to do that anyway.
- ✓ Just because you don't agree with one behavior,
- ✓ It shouldn't stop you from recognizing other good behaviors.

12. Separate the Person from the Behavior

- ✓ It's easy to label a person as difficult or toxic.
- ✓ But if you look closely, it's not about the person, but the behavior.
- ✓ When you separate the person from the behavior,
- ✓ It helps you figure out better approaches to deal with them.

13. Recognize And Ignore Insults

- ✓ Toxic people love to insult others subtly.
- ✓ They will attempt to disguise insults with compliments.
- ✓ It puts seeds of doubt in your mind.

- ✓ Learn to hear the truths behind those veiled statements.
- ✓ And then learn to ignore them.

14. Focus On Solutions, Not Problems

- ✓ Toxic people are the first to place blame.
- ✓ It's easy to do so.
- ✓ What's difficult is to put in the effort to make changes.
- ✓ Be that person who brings the change, even if you're not responsible.

Nurturing your Love Language is Self-Care

CHAPTER 9

"Nurturing Your Love Language Is Self-Care"

"Nature and Nurture Of Love Language"

Each one of us has a specific love language. This love language is imprinted from the womb and nurtured when they are born. There are five love languages. Language based on Quality Time, Service, Touch, Gift, and Affirmation. If we are given expressively when we are young with this love language then we end up reflecting on the favorable expression of values in our relationships. However, if this love language is neglected and abused during childhood, then we can see odd behavioral patterns that can be hurtful to others and ourselves. For example, if a child was not given a gift during childhood he either becomes a miser or will take something without permission just to suffice the overlooked love language.

If a child was neglected with quality time and service, he will end up not giving time and service to his parents in the latter part of his life. He will feel love and comfort only if you serve him and you spend quality time with him.

If you have a child and if he is asking questions over and over again, you must answer them hastily with patience to fill the need for affirmation. That is why some children do not openly talk to their parents because the language of affirmation is neglected during childhood. A neglected affirmation can lose trust and sense of belief in parents or guardians by the child until he grows older.

How we give an affectionate and reassuring touch to our children has an impact on their developmental stage. If we often receive comforting touch during childhood we will always feel secure and loved. But if touch is abused or neglected it has an emotional effect on the child's behavior, as we can see in some battery and violent responses of some adults.

Our love languages and others' love languages can be identified if we carve into our childhood memories and a series of love language tests available on the internet. Recognizing your love language will significantly assert what we are needing, missing, or any inadequacy that needs to be healed and restored. Acknowledging your love language and others' love language is a good tool to better connect with loved ones. Discovering our love languages will promote and facilitate better communication and relationships. It encourages us in offering needs and support for others' growth and our progress as well.

Indifference can't foster in our society if we have seen the necessities that need to be addressed. Commonly we deal with the program of hunger and power but we don't rectify the concern of behavior and human development. That is why all our approaches towards change are a failure because we neglect the heart and roots of the problem.

Each one of us has a specific love language. This love language is imprinted from the womb and nurtured when they are born.

There are five love languages. Language of Quality Time, Service, Touch, Gift, and Affirmation. If we are given expressively when we are young with this love language then we end up reflecting favorable love languages in our relationships. However, if this love language is neglected and abused when we are children then we can see odd behavioral patterns that can be hurtful to others and ourselves. For example, if a child was not given a gift during childhood he either becomes a miser or will take something without permission just to suffice his love language. If a child was neglected with Quality Time and Service, he will end up not giving time and service to his parents as a result of childhood negligence that he experienced. He will feel love and comfort only if you serve him and you spend quality time. If you have a child and if he is asking questions over and over again, you must answer them hastily with patience to fill the need for affirmation. How we touch our children has an impact on their developmental stage. If we often receive comforting touch during childhood we will always feel secure and loved. But if touch is abused or neglected it has an emotional effect on the child's behavior, as we can see in some battery and violent reactions of some adults.

Learning and knowing our love languages and other's love languages can be identified if we excavate into our childhood memories and series of love language tests available on the world wide web so that you can truly assert what we are needing, missing, or any inadequacy that needs to be healed and restored. Recognizing your love language and others' love language is a good tool to better connect with loved ones. Discovering our love languages will promote and facilitate better communication and relationships. It encourages us in offering needs and support for others' growth and our progress.

"
Walk with God. Do not be afraid to walk with Him alone. Remember most who started walking with you will not finish with you.
~Ana Rita Reyes
Woman Of Hope
"365 Days"

Chapter 10

Spiritual Life Is Self-Care

God and me. The most important aspect of humans is his relationship with God. A person can't please people without pleasing God first. All our endeavors, hardworks, plans, and dreams will not culminate without the blessing of God. God allows everything, even our downfall, because God gives us free will to choose or the path of His way.

Yes, God allows us to follow our will, but the grace is not there anymore, and the end result is divine wrath or justice. Sometimes we pray to God and we create our own will, we will sometimes feel the euphoric experience as we thought it was from God but at the end, the outcome is not satisfying and sometimes it become disorder, it happened because we create our own way without seeking the divine wisdom of God and will in our life. Whether we prefer to believe in God or not, he remains a loving God, and a God of justice. Thus, it's up to us to embrace Him or to stay away from His care but we know that at the end of the day, the creator has a final say and judgment to His creation.

Loving God is the most beneficial thing that man must aspire to. Without God, grace and mercy is not available. As we are in the trend of modernism, intellectualization, and woke mentality, let us remain faithful, steadfast and believe in God faithfully regardless of what the world is into. God will never change from age to age,

His commandment and teaching is relevant and of importance, His grace and mercy is overflowing for those who seek it, and His divine justice is ready for those who disobey him. We can't blame God for sickness, poverty, and disorder in the world, yes He is good and loving God, why does he allow it? It is because of people's disobedience and sins, because sin, catastrophe and errors enter into this world. Even good people and saints experience suffering, but how you see suffering as an opportunity to grow and to depend on God alone matters.

In these trying times, it is only God who is faithful to His word that He will remain with us until the end of time. People will change, our plans will be sidetracked, but God will never change, yesterday, today, and until the end of time. God loves us and it is not God who is difficult to find, it is us that lose our path.

Relationship with God is about cooperation and to yield. We have to surrender everything to Him, our sins must be repented, our anxiety and worry must be diminished, and our doubt must be placated. As we move toward God, we need to abandon ourselves to Him. It is through prayer that we abandon ourselves to God. Prayer is an act of humility. Humility is a beautiful fragrance of our soul that pleases God, and by prayer and humility God will answer us. As we often caught by concerns, and issues in life, a simple ejaculatory prayer will suffice what we want God to do to us, abandon, be patient and believe that God will help, will give mercy and will transform you

"Lord Jesus, I abandon myself to you, Jesus take over"

Money must be our servant, and as a Master, we need to show prudence, discipline, and detachment from the evil that will cause us when we have a lot of it. We must control our budget and make money as a means of necessity and not our God.

~Ana Rita Reyes

Financial Literacy Is Self-Care

CHAPTER 11

Financial Literacy Is Self-Care

Having temporal necessities and resources is a grace from God. The importance of how to use these resources is a must. Most people have received so much supply but unfortunately in a spur of a moment everything can be taken away. The choice on how to keep that income depends on our wisdom and understanding of the flow of supply and budget matters.

We are not trained how to spend and save. The purpose of saving and spending does not really transcend to us in learning. When you receive money or any resource we need to identify the purpose of these funds. When we don't know how to spend and save our money then disarray will follow. We must remember that funds come to us for a certain purpose and we must always anticipate it. The common mistake is that when we receive it, we spend it right away aimlessly. Aimless spending is the cause of all financial problems.

Saving is a must and spending appropriately is a virtue. When we know how to value money then we are showing prudence and discipline. Prudence is a way of exercising how to give worth for every fund that we receive and the best practice to give worth to it is by investing your money through valuable business, realty, insurance for your health and property, and emergency money for family needs.

Money controls us when we keep spending, giving, and lending it without return of investment or we are using it for luxury, but we control money if we utilize it for necessity and for something that has an investment in return. Life is full of abundance, unfortunately most people lose their fullness because of poor habits and lack of financial literacy.

No matter how big or small money that you have, the quality of exercising discipline is important. Some people do not have huge cash but can live abundantly and some people who have great wealth but suffer from financial crisis and debts.

Debts are good but it must be a practice with prudence. Live within your means and use resources based only on your needs. It is good advice that instead of borrowing money, you must just ask for help so that there would be no more obligation to pay to people you trusted most, and instead of lending money, just offer assistance by sharing a little blessing to someone so that you will be stressed from asking for payment. The dynamics of lending and borrowing depends on the necessity of a person, and as long as it will not burden you and you have the honest capacity to pay and it will not trouble you then that is your preference.

Money is not literally bad, but abusing it will bring us too many shortcomings. Too much of it can make us prideful and greedy, and less of it will give us stress and trouble one after the other.

Good parenting is self-care

CHAPTER: 12

Good Parenting Is Self-Care

If you don't come from a good family (broken and dysfunctional family) at least a good family must come out of you. Breaking the chain of generational curses and sins is the best way to start and raise your own family. Starting a family life needs patience, endurance and courage. Family must be a reflection of courage because every day you need to forgive, understand and to learn.

The dynamics of the family must begin with the leadership of the father and nurturing by mother. When the father is the sole provider of the family while the mother is the encompassing nurturer in the house, kids will be raised with quality, sensibility and a sense of responsibility. Parents are the perfect role models for their offspring. When parents are honest in their ways, the kids will emulate their actions. Failure to express time management, quality moments, lack of affirmation, and love to kids will defiled children's lives.

There are different approach in raising kids, there are no book that can give you guarantee to raise a productive and accountable children, but a good way of showcasing parenting can be seen this way, are you a parents who:

Offer no love, and no discipline?
More love and no discipline?
No love and more discipline?
More love and more discipline?

It all sum-up with what you want to see in your kids. If you don't want your kids to be defended by a lawyer when they become adults (crimes and misdemeanor) at an early age you must protect them by showing more love and discipline. Parents must be good teachers in physical, emotional, mental and spiritual aspects. The leadership of a father can save a child future and the nurturing of the mother can create a wholesome and loving nature of a child.

If we want to break the cycle of chaos and disorder in the family, the quality of parents will bring the quality of kids. Quality can be achieved by virtue, ensuring values, empowering empathy, promoting discipline and communicating faith in God to children.

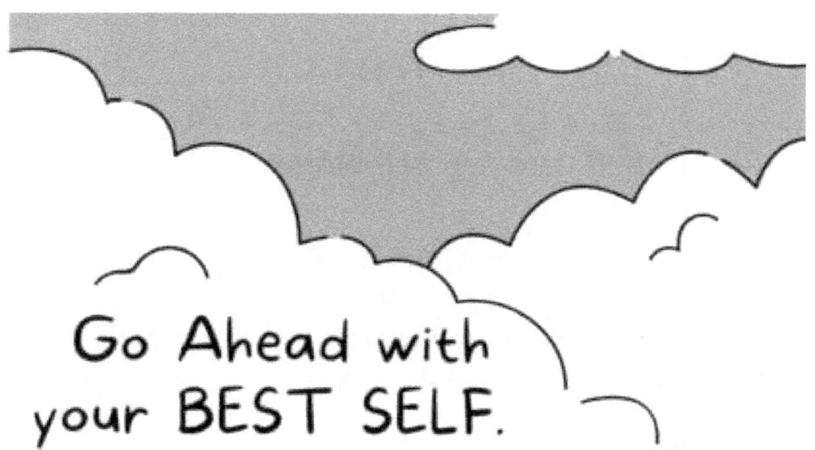

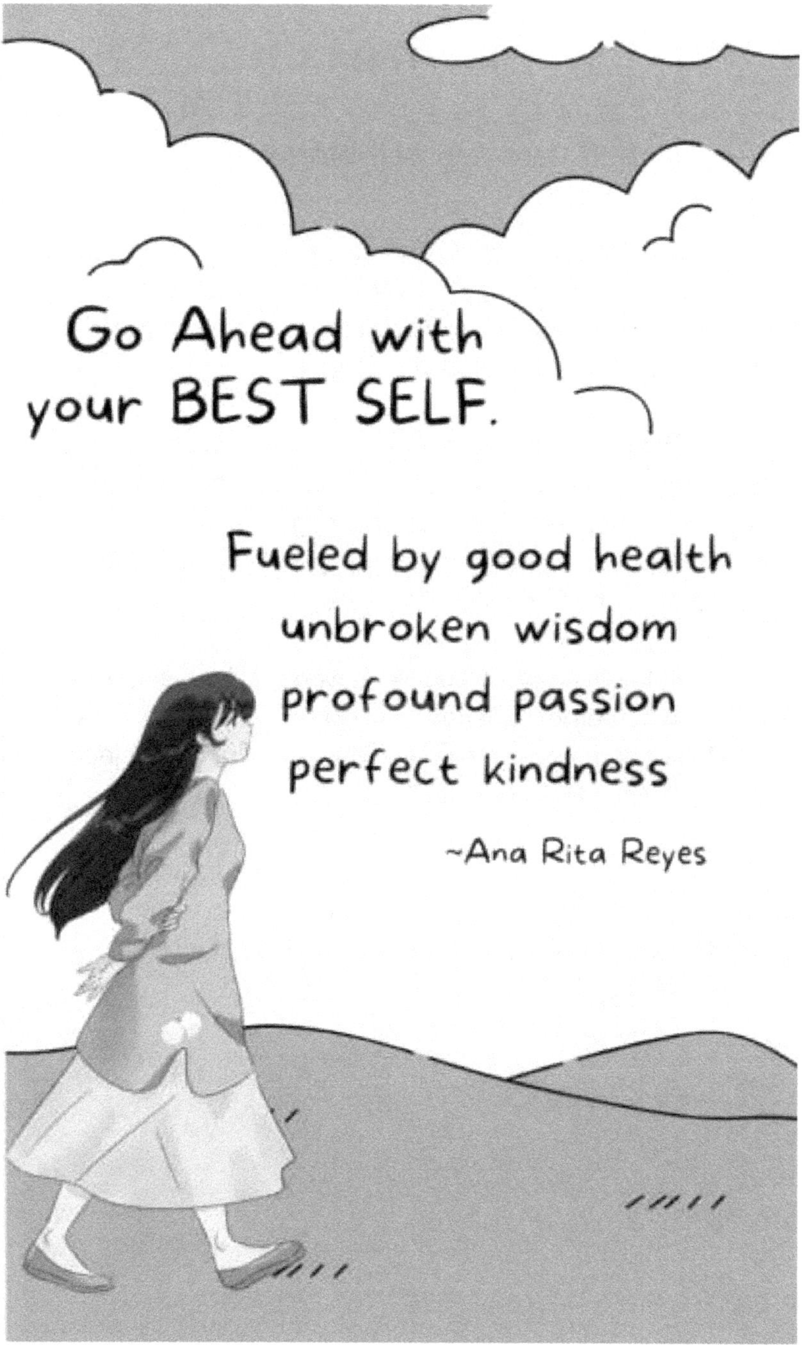
Go Ahead with
your BEST SELF.
Fueled by good health
unbroken wisdom
profound passion
perfect kindness
~Ana Rita Reyes

CHAPTER 13

Self-Care And Self-Worthiness

Self-Care and Self-worthiness are fueled by love. The best way to care and give worth to yourself is to place yourself in the presence of love. The roots of loving others proceed from loving ourselves first.

The practical way to show self-love and self-care is to embark on virtues of gratitude, humility, and piety. This virtue prepares us to walk the path of goodness and righteousness. Our way of expressing love to ourselves must be a reflection of how God loves us.

Self-care and seeing your worth will be achieved by avoiding comparison and ignorance. It simply accepts what is good and helpful for our soul, and it rejects thoughtlessness and insensibility.

Loving ourselves is not selfishness but it is a stewardship of life and our talents that is given to us with the driven purpose of loving Him and serving His people.

Self-worth and Self-care Quotes

Woman Of Hope
"365 Days"

Let us treat people the way God treats us.

@Ana Rita Reyes

Woman Of Hope

"365 Days"

It's not easy to mend a broken heart without fixing first the vision.

Woman Of Hope
"365 Days"
Be thankful to God for helping you outperform all the cares and struggles of your past
~Ana Rita Reyes

Woman Of Hope
"365 Days"

A person glows if peace resides in one's soul.

Ana Rita Reyes

Woman Of Hope
"365 Days"

"

Courage in life is when you learn to move forward and wait patiently.

ANA RITA REYES

Woman of Hope
"365 Days"
The grace to
persevere will
help you
overcome all
obstacle.
-Ana Rita Reyes

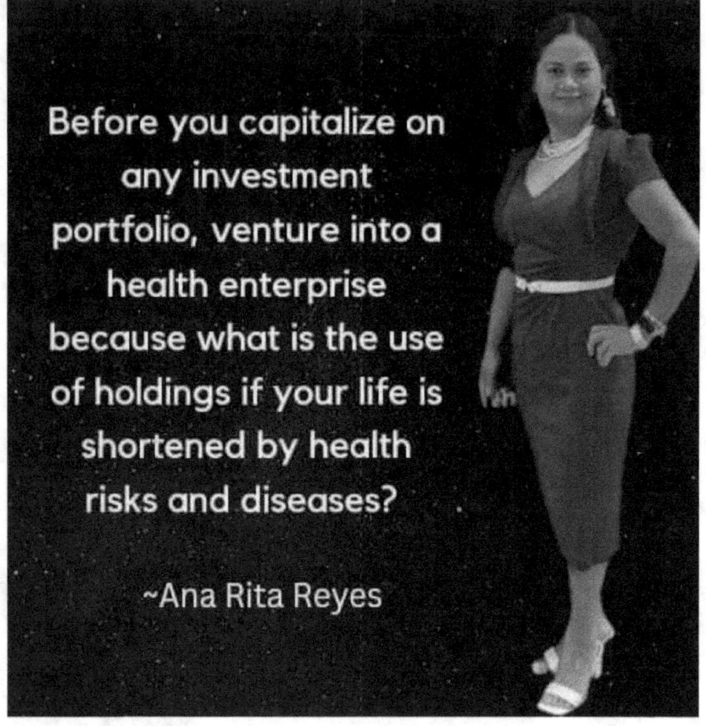
Before you capitalize on any investment portfolio, venture into a health enterprise because what is the use of holdings if your life is shortened by health risks and diseases?
~Ana Rita Reyes

Good health is
a lifetime
commitment to be
fit.
~Ana Rita Reyes

THE AUTHOR WISHES TO ACKNOWLEDGE

This book was made through the inspiration of love and the grace of God. This book will help and give simple directions to people to love and care for their life purposely.

I want to express my love to my husband Randy, and my two boys Joseph and Jericho.

Sending my love and prayers to my Family in the Philippines, my friends here in the USA, Fil-Am SouthBay Community friendship, co-workers, relatives, my great mentors, and the men and women who are hopeful in life.

I like to give value to photos on Canva.com which were used in this book. And the wisdom that I have learned from various authors, saints, and articles inspired me to come up with this self-help publication.

Free Design Tool: Presentations, Video, Social Media | Canva

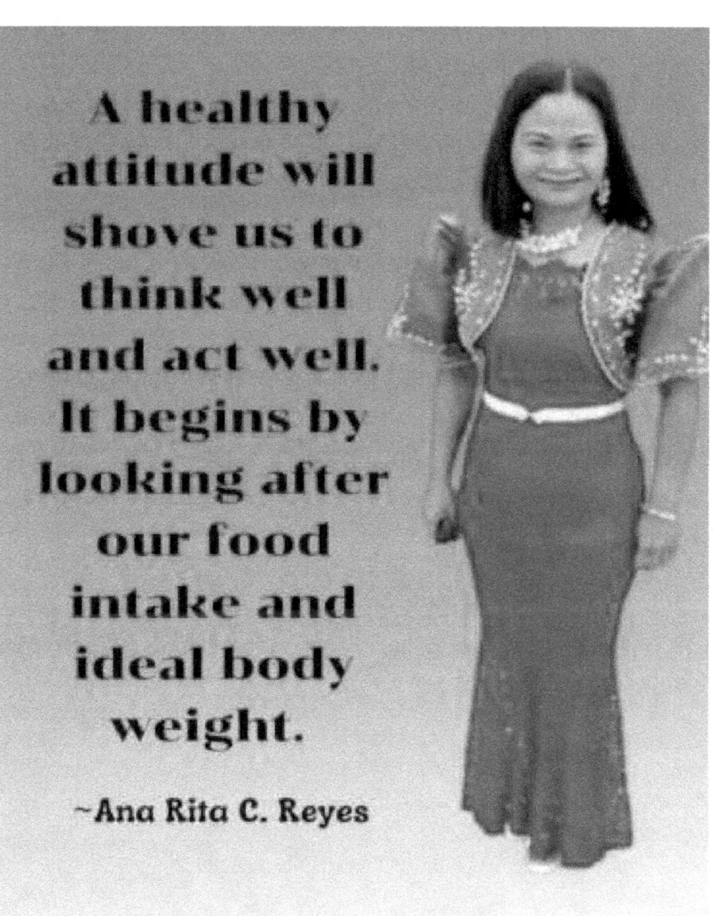
A healthy attitude will shove us to think well and act well. It begins by looking after our food intake and ideal body weight.
~Ana Rita C. Reyes

ABOUT THE AUTHOR

Ana Rita Reyes is an educator, ECE Program Director, Admin of FIL-AM SOUTH BAY COMMUNITY, Commissioner of Library and Education in District 5 San Jose, California, Motivational & Inspirational Speaker, Transformational Life Coach, and a Catechist.

She is been the author of two books. Her autobiography "Woman Of Hope" and self-help book "365 Days"

Her life is dedicated to being a service to the community through service, altruism, and promoting physical, emotional, intellectual, and spiritual change through her blogs and writings on social media and daily Facebook Live inspirational talk.

Her passion and dedication to her career and personal endeavors are driven by love and selflessness for the greater glory of God.

www.ingramcontent.com/pod-product-compliance
Lightning Source LLC
LaVergne TN
LVHW010119170826
845678LV00012B/2497

* 9 7 8 6 2 1 4 7 0 4 6 6 8 *